STEPPING STONE STORIES

Sue Lee
Starts School
by Dr. Lawrence Balter

ADJUSTING TO SCHOOL

Illustrated by Roz Schanzer

BARRON'S
New York • London • Toronto • Sydney

All inquiries should be addressed to:
Barron's Educational Series, Inc.
250 Wireless Boulevard
Hauppauge, NY 11788

International Standard Book No. 0-8120-6152-7

Library of Congress Catalog No. 90-27227

Library of Congress Cataloging-in-Publication Data

Balter, Lawrence.
 Sue Lee starts school : adjusting to school / by Lawrence Balter ;
illustrated by Roz Schanzer.
   p.   cm. — (Stepping stone stories)
   Summary: Worried about starting at a new school, Sue Lee feels
lonely and scared but soon discovers that her natural traits and
talents make her very popular with her new classmates.
   ISBN 0-8120-6152-7
   [1. Self-confidence—Fiction. 2. Individuality—Fiction.
3. Schools—Fiction.] I. Schanzer, Rosalyn, ill. II. Title.
III. Series.
PZ7.B2139St   1991
[E]—dc20   90-27227
                                                              CIP
                                                              AC

PRINTED IN HONG KONG

1234 4900 987654321

Dear Parents and Teachers:

The books in this series were written to help young children better understand their own feelings and the feelings of others. It is hoped that by hearing these stories, or by reading them, children will see that they are not alone with their worries. They should also learn that there are constructive ways to deal with potentially disrupting circumstances.

All too often children's feelings are brushed aside by adults. Sometimes, because we want to protect youngsters and keep them happy, we inadvertently trivialize their concerns. But it is essential that we identify their emotions and understand their concerns before setting out to change things.

Children, of course, are more likely to act on their feelings than to reflect on them. After all, reflection requires tolerance that, in turn, calls for a degree of maturity. A first step, however, is learning to label and to talk about one's feelings.

I also hope to convey to parents and others who care for children that while some of a child's reactions may be troublesome, in all likelihood they are the normal by-products of some difficult situation with which the child is trying to cope. This is why children deserve our loving and patient guidance during their often painful and confusing journey toward adulthood.

Obviously, books can do only so much toward promoting self-understanding and problem-solving. I hope these stories will provide at least a helpful point of departure.

Lawrence Balter, Ph. D.

It was a warm afternoon not too terribly long ago in the town of Crescent Canyon, and summer was just about over.

Sue Lee was playing in the back yard
and her mom was reading.
"Let's go to Chez Kids to buy some clothes for you," said
Sue Lee's mother suddenly. "We'll get you something special
to wear on your first day of kindergarten next week."
"Can I get dinosaur sneakers?" Sue Lee asked excitedly.
"We'll see," answered her mom.

The sun was shining brightly as they walked down
Mercer Street toward Chez Kids.
"Oh, let's stop here at Rivoli Merchandise," suggested Sue
Lee's mother. "There's something I want to get."
"Can I help you, folks?" asked Mrs. Pearl.
"Yes," Sue Lee's mother replied. "Do you have any alarm
clocks?"
"Quite a few," answered Mrs. Pearl with a smile.
"Which one do you like?" Sue Lee's mom asked her.
Sue Lee suddenly realized that the clock was for her.

"I like that one," said Sue Lee pointing excitedly.
"That's a clock radio," said Mrs. Pearl.
"Good choice," said her mom. "The color goes with your
room. And it will get you up for school every morning."
"Anything else?" asked Mrs. Pearl.
"Can I get this? *Please?*" asked Sue Lee pointing.
"And the lunch box, too," said Sue Lee's mother.
"Good luck at school," said Mrs. Pearl as she handed Sue Lee
a big bright pink eraser. "This is for you."
"Thank you," said Sue Lee.

"Next stop, Chez Kids," said Sue Lee's mother.

"How are you today?" asked Miss Lilly.

"Fine, thanks," answered Sue Lee's mother. "We need to get some new clothes for school."

"Great!" said Miss Lilly. "Look around and let me know if you need any help."

Sue Lee tried on at least a million jeans and tops and jumpers.

"Okay," her mother said finally. "I think we've got everything now."

"Bye," said Miss Lilly. "Have fun at school."

"I'm thirsty," said Sue Lee.
"Me, too. Let's stop in at Nifty's Ice Cream Palace for something to drink," suggested her mother.
"Two lemonades, please," said her mom to the waiter.
"Two lemonades coming right up." He winked at Sue Lee.
"Guess what?" her mother suddenly exclaimed. "We forgot to buy the dinosaur sneakers!"
They both laughed.
"Let's buy them tomorrow," suggested Sue Lee's mother.

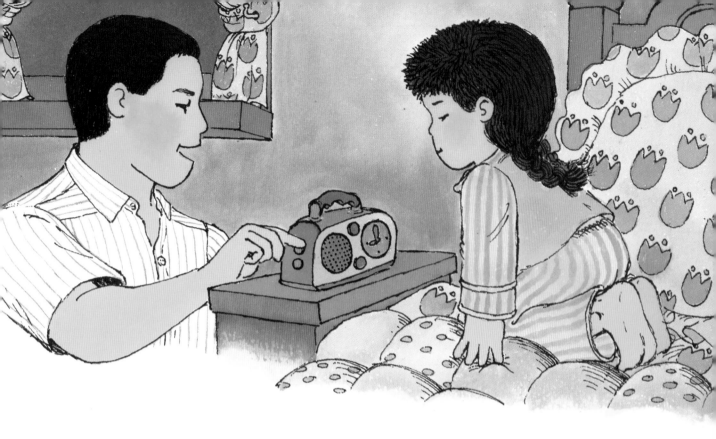

That night, Sue Lee's dad showed her how to set her clock
radio.
"You can listen to music for a few minutes, while falling
asleep," he said. "The radio will shut off automatically.
Then in the morning it will wake you by playing more music."
"Starting tonight, we're going to begin a different schedule
for you," said Sue Lee's mother. "School starts in about a
week. Since you'll be getting up earlier, you'll have to
get used to going to bed earlier, too."
Sue Lee lay in bed listening to her new clock radio.
By the time it had turned itself off, she was sound asleep.

The next day, Sue Lee and her mother passed the school on
their way to buy her dinosaur sneakers.
"You haven't been here since last spring when we came to
fill out the forms," said her mother. "Let's go inside and
see the hallways and the rooms."
"It's big," said Sue Lee.
"At first it looks very big," said her mother. "But when
you get to know your way around, you won't think so."
They walked down the hallway past a lot of doors.

"Here's the principal's office," said her mother.
"Hi," said a woman who was typing. "Will you be starting here next week?"
"Yes," answered Sue Lee.
"I'm Miss Conrad. What's your name?"
"Sue Lee Lin."
"Let's see," said Miss Conrad looking in a book. "You'll be in Mrs. Waterman's class."
"Thank you," said Sue Lee's mother.
"Have a look around," Miss Conrad said with a smile.

"Here's the nurse's office," said her mother. "I guess she's not in right now."

"Why is there a nurse?" asked Sue Lee.

"If any children get sick," her mother replied, "she can look after them until they go home."

"Will I get sick in school?" asked Sue Lee.

"Probably not," answered her mother. "But it's good to know that someone is here, just in case."

"Here's a classroom," said her mother. "Let's see whose name is on the door."
"It says 'M-R-S. W-A-T-E-R-M-A-N,'" said Sue Lee, spelling the letters.
"That says 'Mrs. Waterman,'" explained her mother. "You'll be in her class."
"And here's the bathroom," said Sue Lee peeking past a swinging door. "It has a lot of toilets, like in Mac's Department Store."
"Well, a lot of kids go to the school," said her mother.
"So they need to have room for more than one person."

They walked down the hall together and looked at the decorations on the walls.

"Now that you've had a look around," said her mother, "it won't seem so strange to you next week."

"And I won't get lost," added Sue Lee, squeezing her mother's hand a little tighter.

"That's right. Now, let's get those sneakers you've been waiting for," suggested her mother as they left the school.

Sue Lee felt excited, and a little worried, too.

After buying the sneakers at Chez Kids, they went home.
Dad was already there when they arrived.
"We went to school today, and I got sneakers," said Sue Lee.
"That's terrific," he said. "Let's have a look."
Sue Lee showed Dad her new dinosaur sneakers.
"The school was big," said Sue Lee. "And it had a nurse's
room and an office with typewriters and phones."
"Sounds interesting," said her dad.
"There was a teacher named Mrs. Watermelon," said Sue Lee.
"It was Water*man,*" said her mother, laughing.
Sue Lee spent the afternoon playing school with her dolls.

The next day Sue Lee had a play date at Linda's house.
"I can't stay," said Sue Lee's mom. "I have to go to the
post office. I'll pick up Sue Lee in a little while."
"That's fine," answered Linda's mother.
"No," said Sue Lee suddenly. "I don't want you to go."
"Why not?" asked her mother. "You always stay here."
Sue Lee looked worried and held on to her mother.
"It's okay," said her mother. "I won't go if you don't want
me to."

"C'mon girls. Let's pretend to have 'snack time' the way they do it in school," said Linda's mother. "You get the juice and some cups, and I'll get the crackers."
"I want some peanut butter, too," said Linda.
"I don't want to play," said Sue Lee.
"What's wrong?" asked Sue Lee's mother.
"Maybe she's a little nervous about starting school," said Linda's mom.
"Don't be scared," said Linda. "It'll be okay."
Sue Lee didn't look convinced, and they didn't talk about it anymore while they ate their snack and played.

Later, when they were home, Sue Lee's mom turned to her. "Are you afraid about school?" she asked softly.

"A little," said Sue Lee. "Maybe I won't know how to do things right. And what if nobody plays with me?"

"I'm sure you'll make new friends," assured her mom. "But it's natural to be a little worried, because it's all so new."

"What if I miss you?" asked Sue Lee.

"I'll miss you, too," said her mother. "But, remember, you'll come home every day to Dad and me."

When Sue Lee's first day of school finally arrived, her dad had his video camera ready for action.
"Okay, everybody," he said. "Let's get breakfast on tape."
"I don't feel like eating," said Sue Lee.
"Just take a couple of bites of toast," said her mother.
"I can't," complained Sue Lee. "My stomach feels jumpy."
"It's okay," reassured her mom. "You're probably just a little nervous about starting school. I am, too. You'll be feeling fine by snack time."

They drove to school.

"Wave to me," said her dad as he took more pictures of Sue Lee walking into school for the first time.

The parents were allowed to stay for a few minutes, and then everyone had to say good-bye.

"Have a good time," said Sue Lee's mother.

"Good morning, children," announced Mrs. Waterman. "I think we're going to have a very nice time in school today."
Sue Lee felt a little scared because she did not see anyone she knew.
"Remember to put your things in your cubby when you first arrive," continued Mrs. Waterman. "Then come over and sit down in the circle until everyone is here."
Sue Lee sat in the circle and watched the other kids talk. She felt very lonely.

"Okay, everybody," said Mrs. Waterman. "Come on over to the piano."

Mrs. Waterman played the piano and taught the children a new song to start the day.

At first, Sue Lee didn't know all the words, but she listened and learned them right away.

Next, Mrs. Waterman showed the children around the room.

"Sue Lee," said Mrs. Waterman. "Would you please put some lettuce in the gerbil's cage? Jeremiah looks hungry."

The class did a lot of other fun things during that first
day in school, too.
Some of the kids built with blocks. Others copied numbers.
Heather and Robby knew each other, and they played together.
While she was doing a puzzle by herself, Sue Lee thought of
home, and she began to miss her room and her parents.
"Good job, Sue Lee," Mrs. Waterman said, putting her hand on
Sue Lee's shoulder. "You got the puzzle just right."
Sue Lee felt proud, but still a little lonely.

At story time, all the kids scrambled to sit next to Mrs. Waterman, and Sue Lee didn't know where she should go. Robby and Heather were closest to Mrs. Waterman. "Make a place for Sue Lee, please," Mrs. Waterman said. While Mrs. Waterman read from the book, Heather and Robby giggled with one another.

After story time, Sue Lee put on a smock and started to paint at an easel.

She began with a bright yellow sun, a deep blue sky, a thick field of green grass below, and then she painted a funny purple dinosaur like the one on her sneakers.

"That's lovely," said Mrs. Waterman.

Heather and Robby skipped over and stopped.

"Let's paint," suggested Robby standing at the next easel.

"I don't have any purple paint," said Heather.

"You can borrow some from Sue Lee," suggested Mrs. Waterman.

"I can't give you any," said Sue Lee.

"Sue Lee won't give us any," complained Heather and Robby.
"Sue Lee. Please share your supplies," said Mrs. Waterman.
"But I don't have a jar of purple paint," said Sue Lee.
"Not true," said Heather.
"Yeah!" agreed Robby. "You did a purple dinosaur."
Sue Lee felt upset because they did not believe her.
Before Sue Lee could explain, Mrs. Waterman came over to take a closer look.
Then she spoke.

"I think Sue Lee has something to teach everyone here," said Mrs. Waterman. "Why don't you show the class how you got the purple for the dinosaur."
Sue Lee felt a little shy.
"Well, first I took some blue from the sky. Then I took some red from the jar. When I mush them together, it's purple for the dinosaur."
"Can I try?" asked Robby immediately.
"Show me," said Heather.

Soon everyone had gathered around Sue Lee's easel.
"Can you make any other colors?" Mrs. Waterman asked.
"If you put some blue from the sky with some yellow, it
turns green," explained Sue Lee. "That's how I made the
grass."
Sue Lee felt very happy to have everyone interested in what
she had done.

After the painting lesson, it was time to clean up.
"Okay, everybody," said Mrs. Waterman. "When everything is put away we can line up over here to go home."
Sue Lee put away her smock and washed her hands.
Then she got her things from her cubby and got in line.
"Sue Lee," called a voice. "Stand next to me."
Sue Lee turned around.
It was Heather.
Sue Lee smiled and stepped in line to be next to her new friend.

Sue Lee's mother was right outside, waiting to pick her up.
"How was school?" she asked on their way home.
"I liked it a little, and I didn't like it a little!" Sue
Lee explained.
"I can understand that," said her mother.

"I liked the songs and the toys, and mostly the painting,"
said Sue Lee. "And I think some of the kids liked me."
Then Sue Lee gave her mother the painting she had made.
"It's beautiful," said her mom. "Thank you!"

That night, after her father set her clock radio and kissed her good-night, Sue Lee thought about her next day at school. She would see Heather and her other new friends. Maybe she would build a tower with the large blocks, and even get to knock them down.

She might make another colorful painting to bring home. And, as she drifted off to sleep, the nighttime sky all over Crescent Canyon turned a wonderful shade of dinosaur purple.

About This Book

Starting school is a major step for any child. Independence, which implies having to think and fend for oneself, can be liberating and scary at the same time. Some take to it more easily than others, but it represents an important achievement for all children.

At school, children meet people who have different ways of doing things from Mom and Dad and the few close friends and relatives with whom they are familiar. They notice that other people have different tastes, attitudes, habits, interests, and knowledge. They begin to see that there are options they never before considered.

In addition to social learning, obviously there are important intellectual and physical opportunities at school. Schools can provide scaled-down equipment for children to learn new skills. Children do not have to worry about making mistakes or accidentally damaging the objects they are learning to use.

Most children have some concerns about going off to school. The most common are associated with separation from their familiar home and family. The anticipation of being away from home can pose a threat to their still delicate sense of emotional security.

Many children worry that they will be forgotten. Some are fearful that their parents will not come back to pick them up. If they travel by bus, some children are concerned that the bus will deliver them to the wrong place.

Occasionally, children are annoyed that they will be excluded from their parents' activities while they are at school. It is as though parents are supposed to remain idly in one spot, and only when the children return home from school should life resume for everyone. When there is a new baby at home, a child's sense of exclusion can be particularly poignant.

Parents, of course, may experience separation anxiety, too. It is important to be aware of any mixed feelings about your child's growing independence. An otherwise cheerful youngster can become needlessly anxious about going to school if a parent unwittingly conveys ambivalence.

Preparation is the key to a successful school experience. Knowing what to expect is vital. A visit to the school is an important step in orienting a child. Pretend games at home in which school activities are practiced, are also very useful. Of course, children should be encouraged to express their concerns openly. As parents, we must make every effort to answer their questions seriously and concretely.

In this story, Sue Lee worries about starting a new school. Although she has been prepared in advance, she feels lonely and scared. Despite her apprehension, Sue Lee courageously begins to acquaint herself with her new environment. A misunderstanding unexpectedly occurs on her first day. By being herself, Sue Lee happily discovers that her natural talents and traits make her a very popular and sought after child among her new friends.